HOT RIDES

Written by Matt Crossick

Design by Blue Sunflower Creative

This edition published by Parragon in 2009

Parragon
Queen Street House
4 Queen Street
Bath BA1 1HE, UK

ISBN 978-1-4075-7504-9

Printed in China

HOT RIDES

LIVE. LEARN. DISCOVER.

Bath · New York · Singapore · Hong Kong · Cologne · Delhi · Melbourne

WHAT'S ON THE PAGE

The pages of this book are packed with super stats, fantastic facts and, of course, awesome wheels. Here's what you'll find on each page!

Car name

Introduction

Cool Rating: This tells you how good a car looks. If it makes you go "WOW!" when it drives past, it's a 10. If it looks boring, it's a 0.

Rareness Rating: This tells you how likely you are to see one of these cars.

MITSUBISHI EVO IX

Mean Machine

Car modifiers love this car because it's mean-looking, fast and gives you supercar acceleration for half the price. It uses a turbo for extra power.

Discovery Rating
Cool Rating: 8/10
Rareness Rating: 7/10

Watch out for bonus pages of jokes, quizzes and activities!

DiscoveryFact™: Check out weird and wonderful facts about the cars here!

Visual key: The cool visual key at the top right of each page is a quick reference telling you what type of car you're looking at. The Mitubishi Evo 1X is a road racer.

Hot Road Car: A cool everyday car.

Luxury Cruiser: For luxury rather than speed.

Crazy Car: Crazy machines that are barely cars at all!

Road Racer: Smaller and cheaper than supercars, but still very fast.

Supercars: The fastest, coolest, most expensive road cars money can buy.

Fact File

P SPEED: 157 mph
60 MPH: 4 sec
OWER: 266 hp
NGINE SIZE: 2-liter
NGINE TYPE: 4-cylinder twin
urbo
TORQUE: 289 lb/ft
LENGTH: 179 in
WIDTH: 70 in
HEIGHT: 57 in
WEIGHT: 3,086 lbs
MADE IN: Japan
YEARS BUILT: 2006 onwards
PRICE: ❷

eryFact™

original Lancer
cars were based
Mitubishi's rally
s, which competed
he World Rally
ampionship. They
re originally only
ailable in Japan.

Special Features:
- 4-wheel drive
- Spoiler helps cornering at speed
- Racing "bucket" seats inside

Special Features:
The awesome features that make this car unlike any other.

Fact File Decoder

TOP SPEED: What's the fastest speed this car can do?

0-60 MPH: How quickly can it hit 60 mph from a standing start?

POWER: How strong its engine is.

ENGINE SIZE: Generally, bigger = more powerful.

ENGINE TYPE: How many cylinders it has and how they're arranged.

TORQUE: This is how much pulling power a car has.

LENGTH/WIDTH/HEIGHT/WEIGHT: Show you how big and heavy a car is

MADE IN: Country of manufacture (also shown as a flag clipped to the top of file)

YEARS BUILT: When the latest model of the car was launched.

PRICE: Each car is rated between ❶ (a car an ordinary family might buy) and ❺ (only for multi-millionaires!).

ASTON MARTIN V8

V8 Vehicle

This speedy supercar has a mighty V8 engine to power it along, and sleek looks to match!

DiscoveryFact™

Though this is a new model, Aston Martin has been making V8 Vantages since 1977!

Special Features:

- Brand new Aston Martin engine
- Leather, two-seat interior
- Famous Aston Martin front grille

Fact File

TOP SPEED: 175 mph
0-60 MPH: 4.9 sec
POWER: 380 hp
ENGINE SIZE: 4.2-liter
ENGINE TYPE: V8
TORQUE: 302.4 lb/ft
LENGTH: 184 in
WIDTH: 73 in
HEIGHT: 49 in
WEIGHT: 3,594 lbs
MADE IN: UK
YEARS BUILT: 2005 onwards
PRICE: ❸

Discovery Rating
Cool Rating: 8/10
Rareness Rating: 8/10

ASTON MARTIN VANQUISH

License to Thrill

This scorchin' supercar is so cool it was featured in a James Bond movie as 007's car. Of course, the normal version doesn't have rockets installed!

Discovery Rating
Cool Rating: 10/10
Rareness Rating: 9/10

Special Features:

- Fastest Aston Martin road car ever
- Paddle-shift gears
- Top speed is 10 mph faster than standard Vanquish

DiscoveryFact™

Each Vanquish S takes over 800 hours to build. Most of it is done by hand—even shaping the body panels!

Fact File

TOP SPEED: 201 mph
0-60 MPH: 4.7 sec
POWER: 520 hp
ENGINE SIZE: 6-liter
ENGINE TYPE: V12
TORQUE: 425 lb/ft
LENGTH: 184 in
WIDTH: 76 in
HEIGHT: 52 in
WEIGHT: 4,012 lbs
MADE IN: UK
YEARS BUILT: 2001-2007
PRICE: ❹

AUDI TT QUATTRO

Everyday Excitement

Keep your eyes open for these cool-looking motors as there are lots of them around. The V6 engine makes them faster than your average car.

DiscoveryFact™

Audi was one of the first car companies to use 4-wheel drive, way back in 1980.

Special Features:

- 4-wheel drive
- 6-speed gearbox
- Speed limited to 155 mph for safety

Fact File

TOP SPEED: 155 mph
0-60 MPH: 5.7 sec
POWER: 246 hp
ENGINE SIZE: 3.1-liter
ENGINE TYPE: V6
TORQUE: 207 lb/ft
LENGTH: 159 in
WIDTH: 73 in
HEIGHT: 53 in
WEIGHT: 3,109 lbs
MADE IN: Germany
YEARS BUILT: 2001 onwards
PRICE: ❶

Discovery Rating

Cool Rating: 6/10
Rareness Rating: 5/10

BENTLEY CONTINENTAL GT

Celeb Motor

This luxury cruiser is one of the plushest cars around—which is why lots of celebrities have them parked in their driveways.

Fact File

TOP SPEED: 190 mph
0-60 MPH: 4.7 sec
POWER: 552 hp
ENGINE SIZE: 6-liter
ENGINE TYPE: W12
TORQUE: 479 lb/ft
LENGTH: 189 in
WIDTH: 75 in
HEIGHT: 55 in
WEIGHT: 5,313 lbs
MADE IN: UK
YEARS BUILT: 2003 onwards
PRICE: ❸

Special Features:

- Engine cylinders arranged in a W, not a V formation
- Handmade wood and leather interior
- Paddle-shift gears

Discovery Rating

Cool Rating: 8/10
Rareness Rating: 7/10

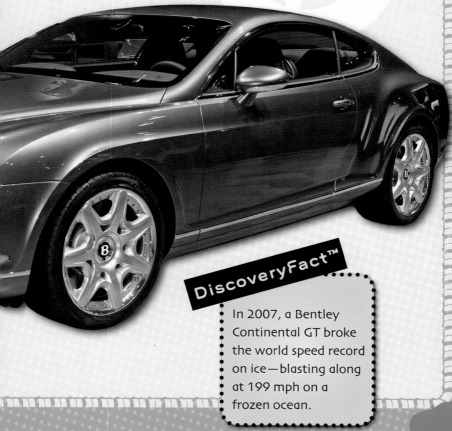

DiscoveryFact™

In 2007, a Bentley Continental GT broke the world speed record on ice—blasting along at 199 mph on a frozen ocean.

BMW M3

Secret Star

This may look like a normal BMW, but it's built for fast driving and quick acceleration, thanks to the chunky V6 engine hidden under the hood.

BMW
M3

Fact File

TOP SPEED: 184 mph
0-60 MPH: 5.0 sec
POWER: 338 hp
ENGINE SIZE: 3.2-liter
ENGINE TYPE: 6 cylinder
TORQUE: 262 lb/ft
LENGTH: 182 in
WIDTH: 71 in
HEIGHT: 56 in
WEIGHT: 3,296 lbs
MADE IN: Germany
YEARS BUILT: 2006 onwards
PRICE: ❷

DiscoveryFact™

BMW has been making M3s since the 1980s. They started out as racing versions of the standard 3-series cars.

Special Features:

- Carbon-fiber roof to make it lighter
- Firm racing suspension
- Upgraded brakes from normal BMW

BMW M5

Road Champion

This is a real supercar hidden in the body of a normal BMW. It's got a massive 10-cylinder engine, and is one of the fastest cars on the road!

Fact File

TOP SPEED: 200 mph
0-60 MPH: 4.5 sec
POWER: 499 hp
ENGINE SIZE: 5-liter
ENGINE TYPE: V10
TORQUE: 383.5 lb/ft
LENGTH: 191 in
WIDTH: 73 in
HEIGHT: 58 in
WEIGHT: 4,255 lbs
MADE IN: Germany
YEARS BUILT: 2005 onwards
PRICE: ❷

Special Features:
- Stiffened bodywork for better handling
- 7-speed gearbox
- 4 seats—a lot for a supercar!

Discovery Rating
Cool Rating: 6/10
Rareness Rating: 7/10

DiscoveryFact™

The M5's engine uses Formula One (see page 40) technology to make it even faster, including hi-tech gears and "launch control" to make it start quicker.

MM 5840

BMW Z4 3.0

Make some noise!

The Z4 has a neat disappearing roof, so you can cruise around with the top down in the summer.

Special Features:

- Speed limited to 155 mph for safety
- Electronic remote-controlled roof
- Specially built new engine for even more speed

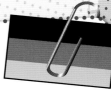

Discovery Rating

Cool Rating: 6/10
Rareness Rating: 5/10

Fact File

TOP SPEED: 155 mph
0-60 MPH: 5.8 sec
POWER: 261 hp
ENGINE SIZE: 3-liter
ENGINE TYPE: 6 cylinder
TORQUE: 262 lb/ft
LENGTH: 162 in
WIDTH: 70 in
HEIGHT: 51 in
WEIGHT: 2,954 lbs
MADE IN: Germany
YEARS BUILT: 2006 onwards
PRICE: ❷

BMW
Z4 M Roadster

DiscoveryFact™

BMW designed the Z4's engine to
be super-noisy, because when you're
driving a fast sports car, you want to
hear the speed as well as feel it!

COOL CAR QUIZ

Test your car knowledge with this tricky quiz!

1. What is the name of this Lamborghini?
a) Gallardo
b) Raging Bull
c) Testarossa

2. How fast can this car go?
a) 32 mph
b) 500 mph
c) 205 mph

3. Why do F1 cars have such huge tires?
a) To look cool
b) For extra grip
c) To help see each other

4. Which country are Ferraris made in?
a) Italy
b) America
c) Sweden

Answers on page 96!

5. Where would one of these be most at home?
a) On a highway
b) In a field
c) On the race track

BUGATTI VEYRON

Extreme Excitement

This is the fastest road car in the world, and one of the most extreme supercars ever built. Just look at that top speed! And that price rating!

Discovery Rating
Cool Rating: 10/10
Rareness Rating: 10/10

Special Features:

- Four turbos to give it incredible power
- 10 radiators needed to cool it down
- 4-wheel drive to harness all that engine power

Fact File

TOP SPEED: 253 mph
0-60 MPH: 2.5 sec
POWER: 1000 hp
ENGINE SIZE: 8-liter
ENGINE TYPE: W16
Torque: 922 lb/ft
LENGTH: 176 in
WIDTH: 79 in
HEIGHT: 48 in
WEIGHT: 4,162 lbs
MADE IN: France
YEARS BUILT: 2006 onwards
PRICE: ❹

DiscoveryFact™

You need a special key, and special racing wheels, to drive the Veyron at its fantastic top speed.

CORVETTE Z06

American Idol

The Corvette is an American car with loads of power and a huge engine. In a straight line, it's hard to beat!

DiscoveryFact™

The Chevrolet Corvette has been in production since 1953. They were very famous "muscle" racing cars in the 1960s.

Discovery Rating
Cool Rating: 7/10
Rareness Rating: 9/10

Fact File

TOP SPEED: 199 mph
0-60 MPH: 3.8 sec
POWER: 505 hp
ENGINE SIZE: 7-liter
ENGINE TYPE: V8
TORQUE: 475 lb/ft
LENGTH: 175 in
WIDTH: 76 in
HEIGHT: 49 in
WEIGHT: 3,126 lbs
MADE IN: U.S.
YEARS BUILT: 2006 onwards
PRICE: ❷

Special Features:

- Available in coupe and convertible
- Supercar performance
- Aluminum frame makes it light

DODGE VIPER SRT-10

Extravagant Engine

American cars are famous for having huge engines, and this one is no exception. Its enormous V10 is one of the largest motors on the road!

DiscoveryFact™

The Viper doesn't have all-wheel drive, traction control or other high-tech supercar features. It just has a huge engine in a small, light body!

Fact File

TOP SPEED: 190 mph
0-60 MPH: 4.7 sec
POWER: 500 hp
ENGINE SIZE: 8.2-liter
ENGINE TYPE: V10
TORQUE: 525 lb/ft
LENGTH: 176 in
WIDTH: 75 in
HEIGHT: 48 in
WEIGHT: 3,408 lbs
MADE IN: U.S.
YEARS BUILT: 2003 onwards
PRICE: ❷

Discovery Rating
Cool Rating: 8/10
Rareness Rating: 9/10

Special Features:

- Rear-wheel drive
- Extra-wide rear tires for grip
- Fold-down roof for summertime driving!

FERRARI ENZO

Slick Supercar

One of the fastest Ferrari road cars ever, the Enzo has the looks to match. Plus it uses F1 technology in the engine!

Special Features:

- Formula-One-style gears (see page 40)
- Carbon-fiber body is extra lightweight
- Big air intakes on the front help it grip the road

DiscoveryFact™

The car is named after the founder of the Ferrari company Enzo Ferrari, who died in 1988.

Fact File

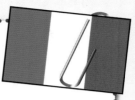

TOP SPEED: 217 mph
0-60 MPH: 3.4 sec
POWER: 660 hp
ENGINE SIZE: 6-liter
ENGINE TYPE: V12
TORQUE: 485 lb/ft
LENGTH: 185 in
WIDTH: 80 in
HEIGHT: 45 in
WEIGHT: 3,020 lbs
MADE IN: Italy
YEARS BUILT: 2003
PRICE: ❹

Discovery Rating
Cool Rating: 10/10
Rareness Rating: 10/10

FERRARI F430

Rev it up!

If you see one of these, keep your ears as well as your eyes open. Ferraris sound awesome when they rev up—just listen to that loud V8 engine!

Discovery Rating
Cool Rating: 9/10
Rareness Rating: 7/10

Special Features:

- Hard-top and convertible models
- A button on the steering wheel changes how the suspension, gears, and handling behave while you're driving.

Fact File

TOP SPEED: 196 mph
0-60 MPH: 4 sec
POWER: 483 hp
ENGINE SIZE: 4.3-liter
ENGINE TYPE: V8
TORQUE: 470 lb/ft
LENGTH: 178 in
WIDTH: 76 in
HEIGHT: 48 in
WEIGHT: 3,197 lbs
MADE IN: Italy
YEARS BUILT: 2005 onwards
PRICE: ❸

DiscoveryFact™

There's a special stripped-out racing version of the Ferrari F430, called the Scuderia. It is lighter and faster than the road car, and built for the track!

FERRARI 612

Speed and comfort

This Ferrari is built for luxury cruising as well as speed. It's the only current Ferrari that has four seats in it, and has a comfy interior rather than a stripped-out one.

Fact File

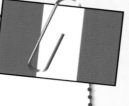

TOP SPEED: 199 mph
0-60 MPH: 4.1 sec
POWER: 540 hp
ENGINE SIZE: 5.7-liter
ENGINE TYPE: V12
TORQUE: 434 lb/ft
LENGTH: 193 in
WIDTH: 77 in
HEIGHT: 53 in
WEIGHT: 4,057 lbs
MADE IN: Italy
YEARS BUILT: 2004 onwards
PRICE: ❹

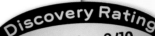

Discovery Rating

Cool Rating: 8/10
Rareness Rating: 7/10

DiscoveryFact™

The 612 is the biggest Ferrari currently made, and replaces the famous Ferrari 474M.

Special Features:

- Body made from aluminum
- Only current Ferrari with 4 seats
- Leather interior

33

CAR NAME SCRAMBLE

Can you unscramble these words to reveal some famous car makers?

1. RIFERAR

2. HGNIRIBMOAL

3. DROF

4. DECSEREM

5. SLOTU

Answers on page 96!

6. NDOHA

7. ZDMAA

FORD FOCUS ST

Speed on a Budget!

Much cheaper than a supercar, but still fast enough to zoom around in. Keep your eyes open for these Fords, as there are lots of them around.

Fact File

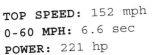

TOP SPEED: 152 mph
0-60 MPH: 6.6 sec
POWER: 221 hp
ENGINE SIZE: 2.5-liter
ENGINE TYPE: 5-cylinder
TORQUE: 236 lb/ft
LENGTH: 172 in
WIDTH: 72 in
HEIGHT: 59 in
WEIGHT: 2,903 lbs
MADE IN: Germany/Spain
YEARS BUILT: 2005 onwards
PRICE: ❶

Special Features:

- Turbocharged engine for more power
- High-performance version of the Ford Focus
- 18-inch alloy wheels

Discovery Rating

Cool Rating: 6/10
Rareness Rating 5/10

DiscoveryFact™

Ford has made the Focus into a rally car, which they enter into the WRC (World Rally Championship) every year—replacing the famous Ford Escort rally cars.

FORD GT

Classic Racer

This supercar is based on a classic Ford racing car from the 1960s with a low, long shape that looks as though it belongs on the race track.

Discovery Rating
Cool Rating: 9/10
Rareness Rating: 10/10

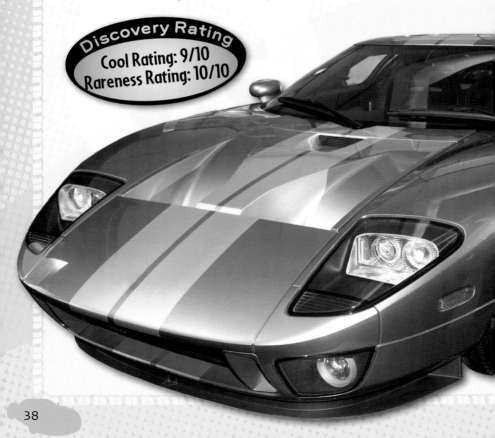

Special Features:

- Supercharged engine for huge power
- Incredibly low body—only 3 feet 8 inches tall
- Engine cover lifts off for easy access

DiscoveryFact™

The original GT40 racing cars, which the new Ford GT is based on, won the Le Mans 24-hour endurance race four times in a row in the late 1960s.

Fact File

TOP SPEED: 205 mph
0-60 MPH: 3.5 sec
POWER: 550 hp
ENGINE SIZE: 5.4-liter
ENGINE TYPE: Supercharged V8
TORQUE: 500 lb/ft
LENGTH: 183 in
WIDTH: 77 in
HEIGHT: 44 in
WEIGHT: 3,391 lbs
MADE IN: U.S.
YEARS BUILT: 2005-2006
PRICE: ❸

FORMULA ONE CAR

Radical Racing

Formula One cars are the most extreme cars on the planet. They accelerate at lightning speed, brake even faster and cost millions to build.

Special Features:

- Incredibly aerodynamic shape helps speed
- Fins and spoilers help car stick to track
- Incredibly high revs, up to 20,000 rpm

Fact File

WORLDWIDE

TOP SPEED: 220 mph
0-60 MPH: 2.3 sec
POWER: 750 hp
ENGINE SIZE: 2.4-liter
ENGINE TYPE: V8
TORQUE: 200 lb/ft
LENGTH: 179 in
WIDTH: 71 in
HEIGHT: 38 in
WEIGHT: 1,334 lbs
MADE IN: Worldwide
YEARS BUILT: New every year
PRICE: ❺

Discovery Rating
Cool Rating: 9/10
Rareness Rating: 10/10

DiscoveryFact™

Formula One cars corner so fast
that drivers can find it hard to
breathe. They have to do special
exercises to strengthen their
necks and stay safe.

HONDA CIVIC TYPE R

Go Customize!

This may look like a normal Honda Civic, but look under the hood and you'll find a more powerful engine and sports-car technology!

RX56 TZC

Fact File

TOP SPEED: 146 mph
0-60 MPH: 6.8 sec
POWER: 198 hp
ENGINE SIZE: 1.9-liter
ENGINE TYPE: 4 cylinder
TORQUE: 158 lb/ft
LENGTH: 167 in
WIDTH: 70 in
HEIGHT: 57 in
WEIGHT: 2,813 lbs
MADE IN: UK
YEARS BUILT: 2007 onwards
PRICE: ❶

Discovery Rating
Cool Rating: 5/10
Rareness Rating: 6/10

Special Features:

- Fast-performance version of the Honda Civic
- Stiffer suspension for good handling
- Lighter than normal Civic, with bigger engine

DiscoveryFact™

The Honda Civic is a popular car for modifiers to customize, because it is small, light, and the engine can be easily upgraded.

HUMMER H2

Monster Machine

One of the biggest cars in the world, you'll know if one of these is coming down your street because the sun will disappear! The Hummer is one HUGE vehicle that is built for off-roading and tough conditions.

Fact File

TOP SPEED: 90 mph
0-60 MPH: 9.9 sec
POWER: 325 hp
ENGINE SIZE: 6-liter
ENGINE TYPE: V8
TORQUE: 360 lb/ft
LENGTH: 190 in
WIDTH: 81 in
HEIGHT: 79 in
WEIGHT: 6,600 lbs
MADE IN: U.S.
YEARS BUILT: 2003 onwards
PRICE: ❷

DiscoveryFact™

Hummer builds the enormous 4x4 trucks that the U.S. army uses in deserts and war zones.

Special Features:

- 4-wheel drive
- Extra-wide for off-road stability
- Protective plates underneath help driving in tough conditions

Discovery Rating

Cool Rating: 6/10
Rareness Rating: 7/10

KOENIGSEGG CCR

Swedish Delight

An extreme supercar from Sweden, the Koenigsegg is a light, incredibly fast car with wicked doors.

Discovery Rating
Cool Rating: 8/10
Rareness Rating: 9/10

DiscoveryFact™

Before the Bugatti Veyron broke the world record, the Koenigsegg CCR was the fastest production car on the planet—hitting 245 mph.

Special Features:
- Aerodynamic shape helps it stick to the road
- Supercharged engine for more power
- Doors open straight up in the air

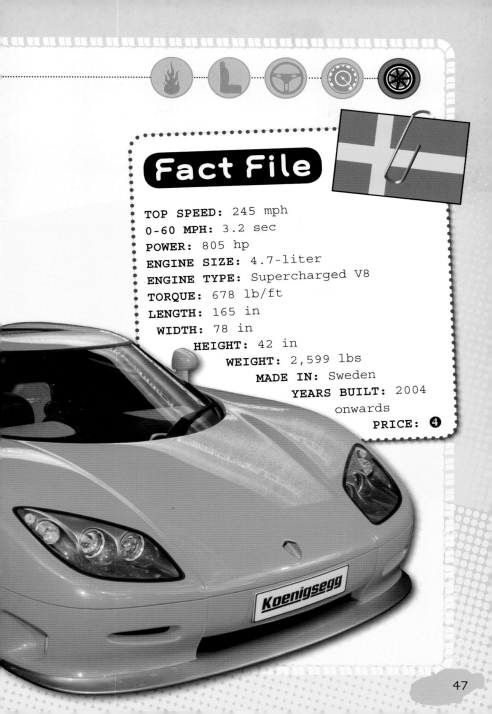

Fact File

TOP SPEED: 245 mph
0-60 MPH: 3.2 sec
POWER: 805 hp
ENGINE SIZE: 4.7-liter
ENGINE TYPE: Supercharged V8
TORQUE: 678 lb/ft
LENGTH: 165 in
WIDTH: 78 in
HEIGHT: 42 in
WEIGHT: 2,599 lbs
MADE IN: Sweden
YEARS BUILT: 2004 onwards
PRICE: ❹

LAMBORGHINI GALLARDO

Brilliant Baby

Smaller than the Murcielago (see page 52), this is the cheapest Lambo you can buy. It can still hit 196 mph, though, and looks absolutely awesome!

Discovery Rating
Cool Rating: 9/10
Rareness Rating: 7/10

Special Features:

- Newly built V10 engine
- Best-selling Lamborghini ever
- 4-wheel drive makes it safe in wet weather

Fact File

TOP SPEED: 196 mph
0-60 MPH: 3.9 sec
POWER: 500 hp
ENGINE SIZE: 5-liter
ENGINE TYPE: V10
TORQUE: 376 lb/ft
LENGTH: 169 in
WIDTH: 75 in
HEIGHT: 46 in
WEIGHT: 3,152 lbs
MADE IN: Italy
YEARS BUILT: 2003 onwards
PRICE: ❸

DiscoveryFact™

Because it is smaller than the Murcielago, the Gallardo has earned itself the nickname "baby Lambo." Not that there's anything small about that top speed!

FIND THE CAR!

Match up the car names on the left with the details on the right!

a) Lamborghini Murcielago

b) Subaru Impreza

c) Monster Truck

d) F1 Car

e) Lotus Exige

f) Ford GT

Answers on page 96!

1)

2)

3)

4)

5)

6)

LAMBORGHINI MURCIELAGO

Scissor Style

This top-of-the-range Lambo has famous "scissor" doors that open straight up into the air. On top of the amazing looks, it can do 205 mph!

DiscoveryFact™

A lighter, rear-wheel drive racing version of the Murcielago, called the R-GT, has competed in several races in the GT300 class.

Fact File

TOP SPEED: 205 mph
0-60 MPH: 3.4 sec
POWER: 631 hp
ENGINE SIZE: 6.5-liter
ENGINE TYPE: V12
TORQUE: 479 lb/ft
LENGTH: 180 in
WIDTH: 81 in
HEIGHT: 45 in
WEIGHT: 3,671 lbs
MADE IN: Italy
YEARS BUILT: 2002 onwards
PRICE: ❹

Discovery Rating

Cool Rating: 10/10
Rareness Rating: 8/10

Special Features:

- Super-cool scissor doors
- 4-wheel drive
- Spoiler can be adjusted for better handling at high speeds

LOTUS EXIGE S

Light As a Feather!

Built for tearing around a twisty race track, the Exige is small and fast. Its small engine is all it needs because the car is amazingly light.

Fact File

TOP SPEED: 147 mph
0-60 MPH: 5 sec
POWER: 189 hp
ENGINE SIZE: 1.7 liter
ENGINE TYPE: 4-cylinder
TORQUE: 158 lb/ft
LENGTH: 149 in
WIDTH: 68 in
HEIGHT: 46 in
WEIGHT: 1,929 lbs
MADE IN: UK
YEARS BUILT: 2006 onwards
PRICE: ❷

Special Features:

- Very light weight
- Supercharged Toyota engine
- Built for the race track

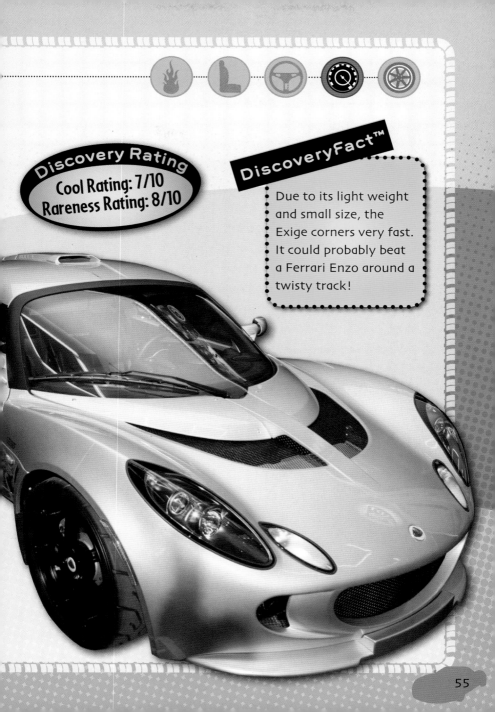

Discovery Rating

Cool Rating: 7/10
Rareness Rating: 8/10

DiscoveryFact™

Due to its light weight and small size, the Exige corners very fast. It could probably beat a Ferrari Enzo around a twisty track!

MAZDA RX-8

Cool Road Car

A sports car for the road, lots of people modify the RX-8 to make them even faster. Custom body panels and upgraded engines make these Mazdas even cooler.

Discovery Rating
Cool Rating: 6/10
Rareness Rating: 5/10

Special Features:

- Back doors hinged at the back—the opposite way from normal car doors
- Carbon-fiber driveshaft reduces weight

Fact File

TOP SPEED: 146 mph
0-60 MPH: 6.2 sec
POWER: 227 hp
ENGINE SIZE: 1.3-liter
ENGINE TYPE: 4-cylinder
TORQUE: 159 lb/ft
LENGTH: 174 in
WIDTH: 70 in
HEIGHT: 53 in
WEIGHT: 2,976 lbs
MADE IN: Japan
YEARS BUILT: 2002 onwards
PRICE: ❶

457MTC

DiscoveryFact™

In 2004, Mazda created a version of the car that ran on hydrogen, instead of gasoline—much better for the environment.

MERCEDES F1

This supercar has crazy doors and a monster engine under the hood. It's also got a hefty price tag!

Fact File

TOP SPEED: 208 mph
0-60 MPH: 3.8 sec
POWER: 617 hp
ENGINE SIZE: 5.4-liter
ENGINE TYPE: Supercharged V8
TORQUE: 575 lb/ft
LENGTH: 183 in
WIDTH: 75 in
HEIGHT: 50 in
WEIGHT: 3,748 lbs
MADE IN: UK
YEARS BUILT: 2004 onwards
PRICE: ❹

DiscoveryFact™

The driver's seat is in the center, with one passenger seat on each side and slightly behind.

Special Features:

- Adjustable gearbox for comfort or racing
- Whole body made of carbon-fiber
- Doors open straight up in the air

Discovery Rating

Cool Rating: 8/10
Rareness Rating: 9/10

F1 MCL

MINI COOPER S

Classic Cool

It's not super-fast, but it is super-cool. You should see them around town quite often—look out for stylish decals decorating the roofs.

Special Features:

- Small with good handling
- Sports Kit option adds stiffer suspension for fast driving
- Hood intake cools air going into engine

Fact File

TOP SPEED: 140 mph
0-60 MPH: 6.9 sec
POWER: 172 hp
ENGINE SIZE: 1.5-liter
ENGINE TYPE: 4-cylinder
TORQUE: 163 lb/ft
LENGTH: 144 in
WIDTH: 76 in
HEIGHT: 55 in
WEIGHT: 2,491 lbs
MADE IN: UK
YEARS BUILT: 2002 onwards
PRICE: ❶

Discovery Rating
Cool Rating: 7/10
Rareness Rating: 3/10

DiscoveryFact™

The old-style original Mini was one of the most popular cars in the world. It was made from 1959 to 2000. The new car is bigger, but keeps some of the old Mini's cool looks.

MITSUBISHI EVO IX

Mean Machine

Car modifiers love this car because it's mean-looking, fast and gives you supercar acceleration for half the price. It uses a turbo for extra power.

Discovery Rating
Cool Rating: 8/10
Rareness Rating: 7/10

Fact File

TOP SPEED: 157 mph
0-60 MPH: 4 sec
POWER: 266 hp
ENGINE SIZE: 2-liter
ENGINE TYPE: 4-cylinder twin turbo
TORQUE: 289 lb/ft
LENGTH: 179 in
WIDTH: 70 in
HEIGHT: 57 in
WEIGHT: 3,086 lbs
MADE IN: Japan
YEARS BUILT: 2006 onwards
PRICE: ❷

HX05
BGV

DiscoveryFact™

The original Lancer Evo cars were based on Mitsubishi's rally cars, which competed in the World Rally Championship. They were originally only available in Japan.

Special Features:

- 4-wheel drive
- Spoiler helps cornering at speed
- Racing "bucket" seats inside

CAR JOKES!

What do you do if you see a spaceman?
Park in it, man!

Why did the racecar ruin the movie for the audience?
Because it had a spoiler!

Why did the driver steer his car into the river?
It was a Ford!

Why did the driver drive his truck off the cliff?
He wanted to test the air brakes!

Why did the driver need a microscope to see his car?
He owned a Mini!

What car can you buy in a flower shop?
A Lotus!

MONSTER TRUCK

Crunch Time

It's illegal to drive one of these on the road because they're so huge! A monster truck is made for crushing other cars, but they race each other, too. They use special fuel to give them incredible horsepower.

Fact File

TOP SPEED: 80 mph
0-60 MPH: 2.5 sec
POWER: 1200 hp
ENGINE SIZE: 9-liter
ENGINE TYPE: V8
TORQUE: 1100 lb/ft
LENGTH: 216 in
WIDTH: 150 in
HEIGHT: 120 in
WEIGHT: 11,000 lbs
MADE IN: U.S.
YEARS BUILT: 1990s onwards
PRICE: ❹

Special Features:

- Enormous tires to crush other cars
- Each truck is custom made by racers
- Carbon-fiber body means it is lighter than it looks!

DiscoveryFact™

Monster trucks are phenomenally expensive to build, because they have to be hand-made from scratch with expensive custom parts.

NOBLE M12 M400

Do the Twist

A super-speedy sports car that's perfect for racing around a twisty track. It's super-light with a big engine, and can beat some supercars to 60 mph!

DiscoveryFact™

Although it is legal to drive one on the road, the Noble M400 is really built for the race track. It corners fast and has excellent handling.

KN54 YBZ

NOBLE

Fact File

TOP SPEED: 175 mph
0-60 MPH: 3.5 sec
POWER: 425 hp
ENGINE SIZE: 3-liter
ENGINE TYPE: V6
TORQUE: 390 lb/ft
LENGTH: 161 in
WIDTH: 74 in
HEIGHT: 45 in
WEIGHT: 2,337 lbs
MADE IN: UK
YEARS BUILT: 2005 onwards
PRICE: ❷

Discovery Rating
Cool Rating: 8/10
Rareness Rating: 9/10

Special Features:

- Big engine in a very light body
- Aerodynamics keep it stuck to the road at speed
- Extra cooling vents stop engine overheating

PAGANI ZONDA

Fearsome Vehicle

A fearsome-looking supercar with four exhausts and a huge V12 engine. It's fast, noisy, and expensive—everything a supercar should be!

Discovery Rating
Cool Rating: 10/10
Rareness Rating: 9/10

Special Features:

- Carbon-fiber body for light weight and strength
- Futuristic shape helps aerodynamics
- Convertible version available too—for even more money!

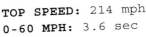

TOP SPEED: 214 mph
0-60 MPH: 3.6 sec
POWER: 602 hp
ENGINE SIZE: 7.3-liter
ENGINE TYPE: V12
TORQUE: 420 lb/ft
LENGTH: 175 in
WIDTH: 81 in
HEIGHT: 45 in
WEIGHT: 2,712 lbs
MADE IN: Italy
YEARS BUILT: 1999 onwards
PRICE: ❹

DiscoveryFact™

The Zonda is a very rare car. They only build about 25 of them every year—so if you see one driving past, make sure you take a photo!

PORSCHE 911 TURBO

Turbo-charged

The fastest 911 out there, thanks to two big turbos boosting its engine power. You can spot a 911 Turbo by its wide rear wing and special body panels.

Discovery Rating
Cool Rating: 8/10
Rareness Rating: 6/10

Special Features:

- Twin turbochargers boost engine power
- Bigger body panels help car stay stable at speed
- 4-wheel drive

Fact File

TOP SPEED: 191 mph
0-60 MPH: 4.1 sec
POWER: 450 hp
ENGINE SIZE: 3.6-liter
ENGINE TYPE: Turbocharged flat 6
TORQUE: 457 lb/ft
LENGTH: 175 in
WIDTH: 73 in
HEIGHT: 51 in
WEIGHT: 3,307 lbs
MADE IN: Germany
YEARS BUILT: 2006 onwards
PRICE: ❸

DiscoveryFact™

Porsche 911s all have their engines in the back, instead of in the front or in the middle. This can make them hard to handle—but it does give them lots of traction.

PORSCHE CARRERA GT

Racer in Disguise

The Carrera is the first Porsche supercar, and one of the coolest cars in the world. It uses Porsche racing technology for extra speed, and has a fold-away roof for open-air cruising.

Discovery Rating
Cool Rating: 9/10
Rareness Rating: 9/10

Special Features:

- Carbon-fiber body for light weight and strength
- Roof comes off for open-air driving
- Uses racing technology for speed and handling

The Carrera GT's V10 engine was originally supposed to drive a Le Mans race car. When Porsche scrapped the idea of a race car, they used the engine for a supercar instead.

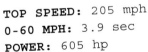

Fact File

TOP SPEED: 205 mph
0-60 MPH: 3.9 sec
POWER: 605 hp
ENGINE SIZE: 5.7-liter
ENGINE TYPE: V10
TORQUE: 435 lb/ft
LENGTH: 182 in
WIDTH: 76 in
HEIGHT: 46 in
WEIGHT: 3,042 lbs
MADE IN: Germany
YEARS BUILT: 2003
PRICE: ❹

PORSCHE CAYENNE TURBO

4x4 and More

This may look like a boring 4x4, but a huge V8 engine under the hood means that it's as fast as most sports cars!

Fact File

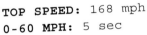

TOP SPEED: 168 mph
0-60 MPH: 5 sec
POWER: 521 hp
ENGINE SIZE: 4.5-liter
ENGINE TYPE: V8
TORQUE: 457 lb/ft
LENGTH: 188 in
WIDTH: 76 in
HEIGHT: 67 in
WEIGHT: 5,192 lbs
MADE IN: Germany
YEARS BUILT: 2002 onwards
PRICE: ❸

Special Features:

- 4-wheel drive, rugged design
- 18-inch alloy wheels
- Big engine makes it as fast as a Porsche Boxter!

Discovery Rating

Cool Rating: 5/10
Rareness Rating: 6/10

DiscoveryFact™

This is the first time Porsche has built an SUV (Sports Utility Vehicle—i.e., a big 4-wheel drive car capable of driving off road). They normally only build sport cars.

TRUE OR FALSE?

1. The Aston Martin Vanquish has featured in a James Bond movie.

2. The BMW M5 is a two-seater.

3. The Bugatti Veyron is a budget motor.

4. The Corvette Z06 is a French car.

5. The Ferrari Enzo uses F1 technology in the engine.

6. The Hummer H2 is a station wagon.

7. The Koenigsegg CCR holds the world's record for the fastest production car.

8. There's a version of the Mazda RX-8 that runs on hydrogen rather than gasoline.

9. You can drive a monster truck to the store.

Answers on page 96!

10. A dragster is the fastest car in the world.

RENAULTSPORT CLIO 197

Hot Hatch

The Clio 197 is a small, fast "hot hatch," with a big engine for its size. These small, nippy cars are great fun to drive!

Discovery Rating
Cool Rating: 6/10
Rareness Rating: 5/10

Fact File

TOP SPEED: 134 mph
0-60 MPH: 6.7 sec
POWER: 194 hp
ENGINE SIZE: 2-liter
ENGINE TYPE: 4-cylinder
TORQUE: 161 lb/ft
LENGTH: 157 in
WIDTH: 58 in
HEIGHT: 70 in
WEIGHT: 2,734 lbs
MADE IN: France
YEARS BUILT: 2006 onwards
PRICE:

Special Features:

- Twin exhausts
- Vents under bumper suck up air and keep car stuck to road
- 17-inch alloy wheels

HK06 UWR

DiscoveryFact™

The Clio 197 is a "hot hatch"—a small, three-door car with a great big engine stuck in the front, and stiffer racing suspension.

ROLLS ROYCE PHANTOM

Silent Luxury

The Phantom is the ultimate luxury car. It's fast but almost silent, glides along on huge wheels and even has an umbrella built into the doors to keep you dry as you get out!

Fact File

```
TOP SPEED: 149 mph
0-60 MPH: 5.7 sec
POWER: 453 hp
ENGINE SIZE: 6.7-liter
ENGINE TYPE: V12
TORQUE: 531 lb/ft
LENGTH: 230 in
WIDTH: 78 in
HEIGHT: 64 in
WEIGHT: 5,478 lbs
MADE IN: UK
YEARS BUILT: 2003 onwards
PRICE: ❹
```

DiscoveryFact™

Rolls Royce also makes a "long wheel base" version of the Phantom. This basically means that the car is stretched, so people inside have more room—perfect for a limo!

Special Features:

- Incredibly luxurious interior
- Very quiet V12 engine
- RR logos on the wheels spin separately—so they're always the right way up!

SUBARU IMPREZA STI

Super Spoiler

Subaru used their rally-car experience to create this fast road car. It's got a turbocharged engine and a big spoiler to keep it stuck to the road!

Fact File

TOP SPEED: 158 mph
0-60 MPH: 5.1 sec
POWER: 276 hp
ENGINE SIZE: 2.4-liter
ENGINE TYPE: 4-cylinder turbo
TORQUE: 300 lb/ft
LENGTH: 176 in
WIDTH: 69 in
HEIGHT: 56 in
WEIGHT: 3,296 lbs
MADE IN: Japan
YEARS BUILT: 2003 onwards
PRICE: ❶

Discovery Rating
Cool Rating: 6/10
Rareness Rating: 5/10

Special Features:

- Road-going version of the rally car
- 4-wheel drive
- Hood intake sucks air into the engine

DiscoveryFact™

Car modifiers often customize Subaru Imprezas, because they aren't too expensive, they're light and they've got really powerful engines.

SUBARU IMPREZA WRX STI RALLY CAR

Tough Stuff

These tough race cars are built for crashing around muddy racetracks. Everything inside is stripped out to make them as light as possible.

Fact File

TOP SPEED: 190 mph
0-60 MPH: 2.5 sec
POWER: 300 hp
ENGINE SIZE: 2-liter
ENGINE TYPE: 4-cylinder
TORQUE: c. 300 lb/ft
LENGTH: 176 in
WIDTH: 71 in
HEIGHT: 55 in
WEIGHT: 2,712 lbs
MADE IN: Japan
YEARS BUILT: New every year
PRICE: ❺

Special Features:

- Car is much more powerful than a road car
- Stripped-out interior completely bare
- Built to drive super fast on mud, dirt and roads

Discovery Rating

Cool Rating: 8/10
Rareness Rating: 10/10

DiscoveryFact™

Subaru has won six World Rally Championship titles with an Impreza rally car. It was one of the first rally cars to use paddle-shift gears.

TOP FUEL DRAGSTER

Demon Car

These are the fastest cars in the world—
but only in a straight line, because they
can't turn corners! They use special fuel
and need parachutes to stop.

Fact File

TOP SPEED: 330 mph
0-60 MPH: 0.8 sec
POWER: 7,000 hp
ENGINE SIZE: 8.1-liter
ENGINE TYPE: V8
TORQUE: 3700 lb/ft
LENGTH: 300 in
WIDTH: about 79 in
HEIGHT: 91 in
WEIGHT: 2,200 lbs
MADE IN: Mostly in U.S.
YEARS BUILT: 1960s onwards
Price: ❹

Special Features:
- Huge rear wheels for massive grip
- Great big spoiler stops car from taking off
- Engine has to be rebuilt after each race

DiscoveryFact™

Top fuel dragsters are even faster than Formula One cars. Drag races take place in quarter-mile strips, and these monsters can cover that distance in under 5 seconds!

TOYOTA CELICA GT

Sleek Wheels

A sleek-looking Japanese road car often modified and upgraded to make it even faster. You can spot one by its sleek curved hood.

Discovery Rating
Cool Rating: 6/10
Rareness Rating: 5/10

Fact File

TOP SPEED: 140 mph
0-60 MPH: 7.2 sec
POWER: 189 hp
ENGINE SIZE: 1.7-liter
ENGINE TYPE: 4 cylinder
TORQUE: 130 lb/ft
LENGTH: 171 in
WIDTH: 68 in
HEIGHT: 51 in
WEIGHT: 2,679 lbs
MADE IN: Japan
YEARS BUILT: 2000-2006
PRICE: ❶

Special Features:

- Faster, cooler version of the Celica
- Lowered suspension for better handling
- 17-inch custom alloy wheels

DiscoveryFact™

The first Celicas were built way back in 1970. They have always been built for fun driving and speed, and have always looked cool, too.

VW GOLF GTI

Zippy Motor

The newest version of the original "hot hatch," the Golf GTI is small and quick. You should be able to spot one of these out on the street.

Discovery Rating
Cool Rating: 7/10
Rareness Rating: 4/10

Fact File

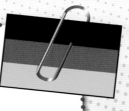

TOP SPEED: 145 mph
0-60 MPH: 6.7 sec
POWER: 197 hp
ENGINE SIZE: 1.9-liter
ENGINE TYPE: 4-cylinder
TORQUE: 206 lb/ft
LENGTH: 166 in
WIDTH: 69 in
HEIGHT: 58 in
WEIGHT: 2,945 lbs
MADE IN: Germany
YEARS BUILT: 2005 onwards
PRICE: ❶

Special Features:

- Turbocharged engine for extra power
- Quick-shifting gearbox for speed
- Small size and big engine make it nice and speedy

DiscoveryFact™

The VW Golf began production in 1974. This latest model is the fifth re-design, and the GTI is the fastest model in the range.

INDEX

ANSWERS

Pages 20-21
1. (a) Lamborghini Gallardo
2. (c) 205 mph
3. (b) For extra grip
4. (a) Italy
5. (c) On the race track

Pages 34-35
1. Ferrari 2. Lamborghini
3. Ford 4. Mercedes
5. Lotus 6. Honda
7. Mazda

Pages 50-51
1. (c) Monster truck
2. (b) Subaru Impreza
3. (f) Ford GT
4. (d) F1 car
5. (e) Lotus Exige
6. (a) Lamborghini Murcielago

Pages 78-79
1. True 2. False 3. False
4. False 5. True 6. False
7. False 8. True 9. False
10. True

CREDITS